CODING IS EVERYWHERE

Coding in Your Home

amazon

BLASTOFF! READERS 2

by Elizabeth Noll

BELLWETHER MEDIA • MINNEAPOLIS, MN

Note to Librarians, Teachers, and Parents:

Blastoff! Readers are carefully developed by literacy experts and combine standards-based content with developmentally appropriate text.

Level 1 provides the most support through repetition of high-frequency words, light text, predictable sentence patterns, and strong visual support.

Level 2 offers early readers a bit more challenge through varied simple sentences, increased text load, and less repetition of high-frequency words.

Level 3 advances early-fluent readers toward fluency through increased text and concept load, less reliance on visuals, longer sentences, and more literary language.

Level 4 builds reading stamina by providing more text per page, increased use of punctuation, greater variation in sentence patterns, and increasingly challenging vocabulary.

Level 5 encourages children to move from "learning to read" to "reading to learn" by providing even more text, varied writing styles, and less familiar topics.

Whichever book is right for your reader, Blastoff! Readers are the perfect books to build confidence and encourage a love of reading that will last a lifetime!

This edition first published in 2019 by Bellwether Media, Inc.

No part of this publication may be reproduced in whole or in part without written permission of the publisher. For information regarding permission, write to Bellwether Media, Inc., Attention: Permissions Department, 6012 Blue Circle Drive, Minnetonka, MN 55343.

Library of Congress Cataloging-in-Publication Data

Names: Noll, Elizabeth, author.
Title: Coding in Your Home / by Elizabeth Noll.
Description: Minneapolis, MN : Bellwether Media, Inc., 2019. | Series:
    Blastoff! Readers. Coding Is Everywhere | Includes bibliographical
    references and index. | Audience: Ages 5 to 8. | Audience: Grades K to 3.
Identifiers: LCCN 2017060000 (print) | LCCN 2018000592 (ebook) | ISBN
    9781626178373 (hardcover : alk. paper) | ISBN 9781618914811
    (pbk. : alk. paper) | ISBN 9781681035789 (ebook)
Subjects: LCSH: Home automation–Data processing–Juvenile literature. |
    Household electronics–Automatic control–Juvenile literature.
Classification: LCC TK7881.25 (ebook) | LCC TK7881.25 .N65 2019 (print) | DDC 643/.6–dc23
LC record available at https://lccn.loc.gov/2017060000

Editor: Christina Leaf   Designer: Brittany McIntosh

Printed in the United States of America, North Mankato, MN

Table of Contents

Do things in your home use **code**? Computers and **smartphones** do.

But washing machines,
vacuums, and lights
may use code, too!

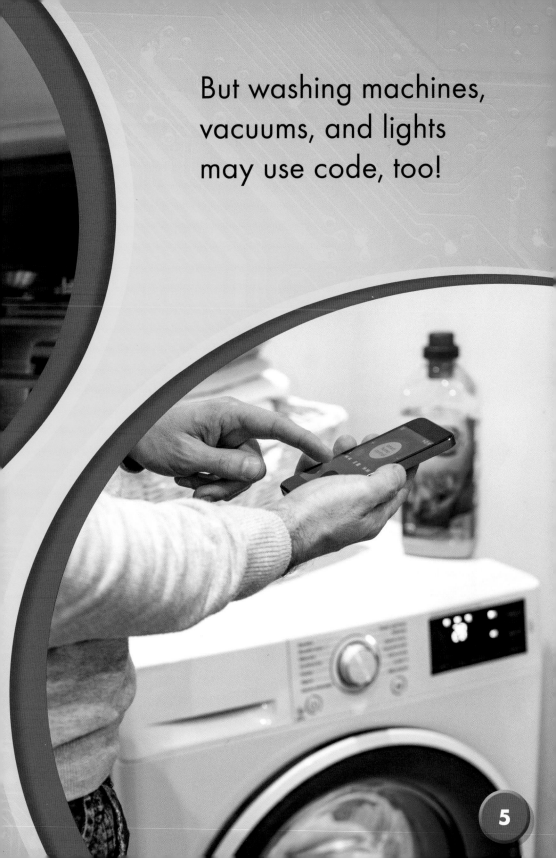

Code is a set of computer rules. It is written in **programming languages**.

```
rgs = {
    a": nestData,
    sgmap": get_locale_msgs(nestData),
    expanded_ids": request.cookies.get("expandedIds", []),
    "sim_snapshot_url": sim_snapshot_url
```

Python code
for Nest thermostat

```
# Generate schedule menu HTML if there are changes to the data nee
if has_prev_content and (diff_list is None or len(diff_list) == 0
    print "No change in top-level API data needed for schedule vi
    sched_html = None
else:
    sched_html = render_template("nestdata_schedule.html", **temp

# Generate API data HTML on each request to show structures and a
ontent_html = render_template("nestdata.html", **template_args)

urn {"content": content_html, "schedule": sched_html}


    era_imgs(camera_id, camera):
    ns HTML generated from Jinja2 templates.  Looks for save
        istory view.

            store.get_device_file_paths('cameras', '{0}.jpg

            rsed(sorted(hist_files.items(), key=lam
```

These include **Java** and **Python**.

Roomba

How is code used in homes?
Roombas use code to know when
and where to vacuum.

An Echo uses code
to order supplies.
Siri uses code to
play music.

Echo

The History of Coding in Homes

inside
ECHO IV

In 1966, an **engineer** built a computer for his home.

He called it ECHO IV. It controlled some **electronics**. It also made shopping lists!

ECHO IV controller

In 1975, engineers created the X10 system.

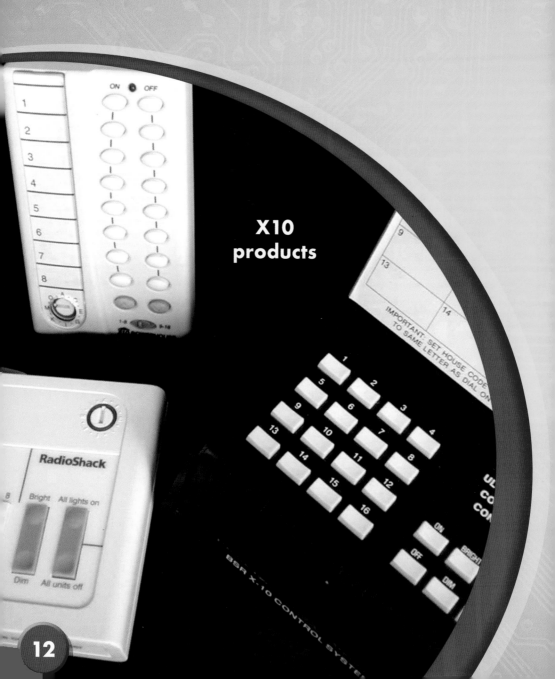

X10
products

It controlled **appliances** and lights **remotely**. This was a big step in home **automation**.

Today, many home devices connect to the Internet. This is the Internet of Things.

Often, people control everything with smartphones.

How Does Coding Work in Your Home?

alarm
system

Many homes have alarms or heat that use code. Code can lock doors when owners are away.

It adjusts heat to save energy. Someday, the whole house could use code!

Setting the Heat

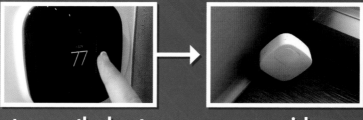

turn up the heat

sensor picks up temperature colder than setting

code tells heater to turn on

room temperature goes up!

A **smart home** has code built into it.

COOL SET TO
70

A central computer connects to the Internet. It controls lights, heat, windows, and more.

Future houses might use **sensors** to recognize owners.

Using code, electronics could adjust right away. What code would you write for your smart home?

Glossary

appliances—electric household items with specific purposes; refrigerators, toasters, and microwaves are all common appliances.

automation—the state of operating without human control

code—instructions for a computer

electronics—devices that use many small electrical parts in order to work; televisions, radios, and computers are common electronics.

engineer—a person who designs and builds engines, computers, and other machines

Java—a programming language that works on many different machines

programming languages—special languages that humans use to talk to computers

Python—an easy-to-use programming language that can build many different things

remotely—from far away

sensors—devices that respond to light, temperature, movement, or other physical changes

smart home—a home with code built in

smartphones—cell phones that are computers

To Learn More

AT THE LIBRARY

Liukas, Linda. *Hello Ruby: Adventures in Coding*. New York, N.Y.: Feiwel and Friends, 2015.

Lyons, Heather, and Elizabeth Tweedale. *A World of Programming*. Minneapolis, Minn.: Lerner Publications, 2017.

VanVoorst, Jenny Fretland. *Robots at Home*. Minneapolis, Minn.: Jump!, 2016.

ON THE WEB

Learning more about coding in your home is as easy as 1, 2, 3.

1. Go to www.factsurfer.com.

2. Enter "coding in your home" into the search box.

3. Click the "Surf" button and you will see a list of related web sites.

With factsurfer.com, finding more information is just a click away.

Index

The images in this book are reproduced through the courtesy of: pianodiaphragm, front cover; Filipe Frazao, p. 4; Dominik Pabis, p. 5; PR Image Factory, p. 6; Brittany McIntosh, pp. 7, 17 (top left, top right, bottom right); Serhii Krot, p. 8; Amazon, p. 9; David Cortesi, pp. 10, 11; Atlant, p. 12; Marko Poplasen, p. 13; goodluz, p. 14; Zapp2Photo, p. 15; Nest, p. 16; Alhim, p. 17 (bottom left); REDPIXEL.PL, pp. 18, 19; Monkey Business Images, p. 20; Alexander Kirch, p. 21.